For my mom, whose occasional jingles were as legendary as her love.
And to Harry, my brilliant boy, the next story is for you.

All rights reserved. No part of this book may be reproduced or transmitted in any form or by any means, electronic or mechanical, including photocopying, recording or by any information storage and retrieval system, without written permission from the publisher, except for brief quotations in a review.

The authors and publisher have taken care in the preparation of this book but make no expressed or implied warranty of any kind and assume no responsibility for errors or omissions. No liability is assumed for incidental or consequential damages in connection with or arising out of the use of the information or programs contained herein.

All trade and product names are trademarks, registered trademarks, or service marks of their respective companies and are the property of their respective holders and should be treated as such.

Without in any way limiting the author's exclusive rights under copyright, any use of this publication to "train" generative artificial intelligence (AI) technologies to generate text is expressly prohibited. The author reserves all rights to license uses of this work for generative AI training and the development of machine learning language models.

First Printing 2025

Copyright © 2025 by Kristen Kehrer

ISBN paperback version: 9781634626965

ISBN hardcover version: 9781634627252

Library of Congress Control Number: 2025932322

SUSiE'S SCHOOL BUS SOLUTiON

A Computer Vision Story

WRiTTEN BY KRiSTEN KEHRER
iLLUSTRATED BY SiNEM KiLiC R.

Every morning, Susie would race,
Out of the house with a frantic pace.
Her school bus came around eight-o-three,
But she missed it too often, and she would agree

Her Mom, a coder with an idea pretty grand,
Said, "Let's solve this problem with a clever plan.
We'll make a system for when the bus is near,
So you can get ready without any fear!"

Computer vision can detect your bus ride,
Ensuring that you'll get inside.
Before we use this to help us out,
Let me tell you what it's all about:

From apps that unlock with just your face,
To self-driving cars that bring you someplace.
A photo filter to make you look like a shark.
Sometimes using cameras that work in the dark.

In hospitals, it lends its eyes,
Spotting areas where danger lies.
Computer vision is a field of AI,
That'll work for our problem, and I can explain why.

SELF DRIVING CARS

BONE FRACTURE DETECTION

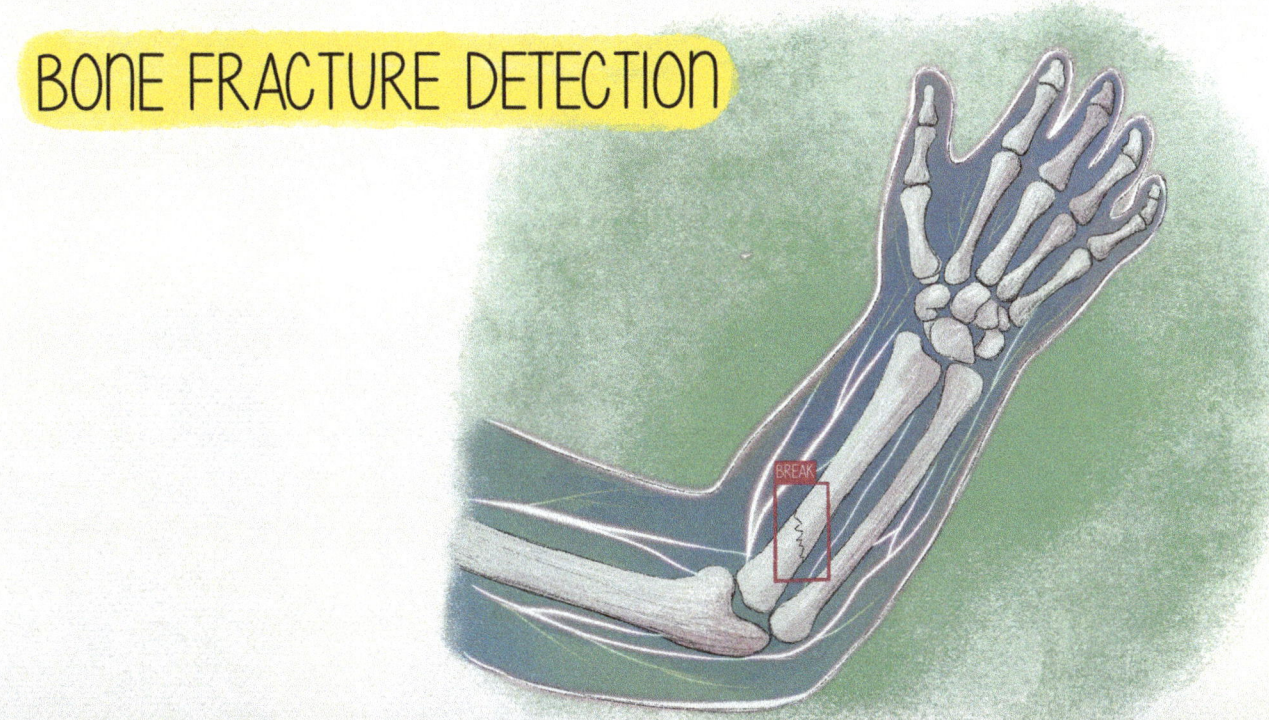

The bus will pass our house not once but twice,
Making it possible to build our device.
If the bus didn't drive past and come back, it would be hard,
We'd only be notified once the bus passed our yard.

Now, let's get started, we'll start with step one.
Building this detector is going to be fun!

"First," said Mom, "the computer will need to see,
What this bus looks like, reliably.
We'll record videos of the bus each day,
As it passes our house on its way."

We can use videos of the bus to teach,
a system to spot when the bus is in reach.
Together we can set up a camera so neat,
Pointed at the road, capturing the street.

They recorded the bus passing for a couple of days.
Saving this video would be the first phase.

"Now we've got video," Mom gave a cheer,
"It's time to turn this video into images, dear.
The more it learns from the patterns it sees,
The smarter it gets, to detect buses with ease."

Next, we label each bus with care,
So the computer knows what object is there.
For alerts to work, the system will need to know,
What the bus looks like in the dark, in the light, and in the snow.

Each image we'll mark with the bus in view,
For this part, you can help, too.

Susie helped with a steady hand,
Drawing rectangles around each bus as planned.

"Here it is!" she'd point with glee,
Marking the pictures with a bus she'd see.

The computer will learn from every clue,
Each labeled image helps it see what's true.
Next, to choose a computer vision model just right,
Consider your goal and the project in sight.

See, computer vision can be used for different goals,
Then Mom listed some of its roles:

Pose estimation models track your every stance,
From your walking steps to a lively dance.
Object models find what's in a scene,
A ball, a car, or something green!

FROG, CAT, DOG, BALL, CAR

Text recognition can read a sign.
And find letters and numbers just fine.
Every model has a job to do,
To help computers see like me and you!

The bus is an object we want our system to see,
We'll choose an object detection model for you and me.

When the model learns new objects, we call that training,
The accuracy improves with the information it's gaining.
Powerful computers are needed to meet this aim,
Using some of the same technology used for video games.

After choosing a model, they set the computer to train
And if it didn't work well, they'd add more pictures again.

Susie watched as the computer whirred,
"What's it doing?" she asked, undeterred.
"It's analyzing the pictures, one by one,
Training itself until it is done."

The system learned the wheels and lights,
The bus's size and it's height.
By the end, the model could confidently say,
"School bus detected." There's a bus on the way.

The trained model is great, it detects a bus with ease,
But without a text or alert, it won't yet meet our needs.
We'll code it to text when the bus is near,
So you'll know when it's time to get in gear.

So Mom started coding, these alerts would be the last piece.
Hoping missed busses would soon decrease.

They again pointed the camera to monitor the street,
To look for the bus's shape and maybe the seats.
As the bus sped past, what came next?
A picture of the bus in their first alert text!

"Your bus is coming! Time to go!"
No more guessing, now she'd know.

The next morning, Susie heard the beep,
And leapt from bed after a restful sleep.
"It's time to go!" her phone did chime,
And Susie got dressed just in time.

From that day on, no bus was missed,
No more rough mornings, with this new assist.
It all paid off, the system was great,
And Susie reached school, never too late.

Susie told her friends about the fun,
What she and her Mom had built and done.
Her Mom gave a hug and smiled wide,
A little effort can give you so much pride.

The world is yours to explore and see.
You can solve problems with creativity.

Glossary:

AI – Artificial Intelligence (AI) is when computers are made to think and learn like people. AI uses a model to make a best choice, then takes an action. The action could be answering your question, suggesting a song, stopping your car, or many other actions!

App - An app is a program you use on a phone, tablet, or computer to do something fun or helpful, like playing a game or watching videos.

Bounding Box - A bounding box is the name for the rectangles we drew around the buses to help the computer learn. The software we used to draw the boxes on images for this project is Roboflow.

Coder - Someone who uses programming languages to give instructions to a computer. Coders use these languages to create apps, games, websites, and more. Someone who has a job coding for work is typically referred to as a software engineer or a programmer.

Computer Vision - Computer vision helps computers 'see' and understand pictures and videos. It uses different tools, called models, to do special jobs. Some models can tell how people are moving (like pose estimation), and others can find objects, like spotting your school bus on the road. Computer vision is one area of artificial intelligence.

Model Training - Training is when we teach a computer by showing it many examples, like showing it pictures of buses so it can learn what a bus looks like. Or giving the models lots of written words so that they can learn the language and answer your questions. After seeing many examples, the model can predict the best response based on the information it has already seen.

Object Detection - Object detection is the type of computer vision where a computer looks at a picture and finds things in it, like a bus, a dog, or a ball, and shows where they are by drawing a rectangle around them.

Pose Estimation - Pose estimation is when a computer looks at a picture or video and figures out how someone is standing, sitting, or moving, like knowing if you're jumping or waving. It is trying to identify how your arms and legs are positioned.

Programming Language - A programming language is how we talk to a computer to tell it what to do. We write our 'instructions' using lines of code. There are many programming languages and each one is like learning a different way to talk to the computer.

Repository - Although this word was not mentioned in the book, a repository is where a person who codes stores their code for safekeeping and to make sure that they're always using the newest version. The repository for the real-life school bus detector is here: https://github.com/KristenKehrer/bus-detector.

Super-Resolution - Super-resolution is a type of computer vision model that makes blurry pictures clearer so you can see all the tiny details better. This has been really useful in making satellite images clearer to understand how melting ice or cutting down trees is impacting our environment.

System - A system is when different parts work together to do a job or task. For example, in the system we built, there's a camera to watch for the bus, a model that has learned what the bus looks like, and alerts to tell you when it's coming. All these parts work together as a system to help you never miss the bus!

Text Recognition - A type of model used to help a computer read letters and words in pictures, like reading a stop sign in a photo.

Reinforcement Learning (That's a pun):

1. Put the steps in order that we used to build the bus detector:
   ___ Trained the model on our bus data
   ___ Turned the video into images
   ___ Gathered video data of the school bus
   ___ Set up text alerts for the bus
   ___ Marked the bus on the images
   ___ Chose an object detection model

2. Draw lines and dots to show what this image would look like if a computer vision model was using it for pose estimation.
Don't worry if your drawing doesn't exactly match the example. Different computer vision models can estimate poses in slightly different ways.

3. Do you think these pictures would help train the object detection model? Why or why not?

4. Do you think you might trick the computer into thinking this is a human? What could you do to help improve the model?

5. Have you ever had an idea for an invention? Can you think of one?

Solution guide for activities

1. Put the steps in order that we used to build the bus detector:
   - Gathered video data of the school bus
   - Turned the video into images
   - Marked the bus on the images
   - Chose an object detection model
   - Trained the model on our bus data
   - Set up text alerts for the bus

2.

3. Do you think these pictures would help train the object detection model? Why or why not?

Yes! Pictures of only part of the object help the model to identify the object when they're not fully visible. Think about the bus driving just into the camera's view, and the camera can't see the whole bus yet. In the case of self-driving cars, the objects that must be detected might be partially covered. Sometimes, the people training these models will create partial images by using techniques to crop the pictures differently and add them to the dataset.

4. Do you think you might trick the computer into thinking this is a human? What could you do to help improve the model?

Yes! If you have a partial image with only the top half of the person, the computer might detect this as a human, even pictures with the tail showing could still be identified by the model as a human. You could train the model on pictures of mermaids to help the model do a better job of identifying mermaids when the whole body is showing.